I0211046

All Saints and
Other American Sonnets

poems by

Jack J. B. Hutchens

Finishing Line Press
Georgetown, Kentucky

All Saints and
Other American Sonnets

ACKNOWLEDGMENTS

Level Land: Poems For and About the I35 Corridor: "The Flesh of Hands"
Sisyphus: "Warsaw"
WordCity Lit: "Lament for Mariupol"

Publisher: Leah Huete de Maines
Editor: Christen Kincaid
Cover Art: Amanda Klousnitzer-Hutchens
Author Photo: Amanda Klousnitzer-Hutchens
Cover Design: Elizabeth Maines McCleavy

Order online: www.finishinglinepress.com
also available on amazon.com

Author inquiries and mail orders:
Finishing Line Press
PO Box 1626
Georgetown, Kentucky 40324
USA

Contents

for Amanda and Harriet

The Flesh of Hands

As a child I knelt in streams cupping water in my hands
seeing how long I could hold it. However tight I pressed
the water seeped through the unseen cracks and creases
between my fingers, and now I know flesh is imperfect.

As a child I cupped my grandfather's hands in mine seeing
how long I could hold them. However tight I pressed
he slipped through the unseen cracks and creases
of eternity, and now I know the flesh of hands has labored long days.

As a man I do not try to cup anything too tight in my hands
prejudiced as I am by childhood. I only watch the unseen
cracks and creases in the flesh of my hands grow
wider and deeper as years pass.

Now at the stream I no longer worry about holding onto anything.
I only run my hands through the water, and the water passes by.

The Old Ford

My first car was a giant of a truck;
my parents' old 1975 Supercab,
long, broad, and loud barreling down
pasture trails, dirt roads, and blue highways.

It wasn't pretty, but it could blow the doors
off any sports car fool enough to come around
our parts looking for a drag down Main Street;
that dog might not hunt, but that thing would move.

By the time I got it, it was hard-driven from hauling
a full cord of wood at a time to get ready for winter,
and banged up from summers of roofing jobs;
it got ten miles to the gallon and fishtailed around corners.

In the end, the front axle gave out, broken by overwork and time,
the truck's demise marking the end of my own reckless adolescence.

The Last Friday Night

my last high school football game
played right after a winter storm
each blade of grass heavy with a clear
thick coat of jagged ice

by the end our young hands were raw
and numb after a long night of galloping
suicidally towards each other
I think that's how Wright put it

that was the last Friday night I had to spend
under the watchful eyes of anxious
townsfolk all praying for bragging rights
to keep themselves warm through the dark year

I believe we won that game, but I can't be sure now thirty-some-odd
years later, nursing early onset arthritis and possibly CTE

Squirrel

That one time we were driving home
after cutting wood for the winter
truck loaded down heavy with a full cord
engine struggling down narrow gravel roads

And, where the gravel meets the highway
we see this squirrel, I swear the size of a small
dog, rooting around for acorns and walnuts
fattening itself up for cold months of sleep.

Pop pulls over, doesn't bother putting it in park,
says "Hey! Hand me that .22!"
engine still humming he leans out the window
aiming, breaking I don't know how many laws.

I often think back to our family eating squirrel for dinner that night,
our relish in meat fatted by sweet acorn and earthy walnut.

My Father Taught Me Poetry

my father taught me the poetry
of hands calloused rough by labor
the even caesura in a well-pitched roof
tied in couplets of clean straight tack welds

he would perform symphonies
in the crescendo of growling chainsaws
on autumn days spent in bare Kansan timber
gathering wood against the fugue of winter

with worn hammer and chisel he sculpted
our sturdy dining table out of lumber
painted thick with six layers of shellac
hard as granite and smooth as marble

all these tools he passed to me in a steel box laden with the burdens
of a worker selling their time at the expense of other endeavors

The Chocolate Easter Bunny

We all start with the ears
though, the weirder among us
will begin with the ass, sheepishly
smiling like it's only a joke.

(Ironically, you can't eat a rabbit's ears,
while the rump is the best part
if braised slowly, with tender care,
salt, pepper, garlic, and carrots.)

On Easter Sunday, the chocolate bunny becomes,
for a brief, reverent moment a kind of communion host,
its body of milk, cocoa, and sugar
transubstantiating as we bring it to our lips.

Later at church in our best pastels, dark lips still sticky and sweet,
we raise our eyes to heaven in awe of their saccharine martyrdom.

Cleaning the Gutters of the Rich

It's not the work I mind,
nor the assumption that I don't read poetry,
or frequent biting winds that leave
my face numb and my hands aching.

It's the 11/12 pitch to the roofs
I'm expected to scramble over
lying flat against rough shingles
hanging on for dear life.

But the tall glimpses I get of bare
autumn trees cracking in the cold
and green backyards that slope down
to gentle streams, remind me of childhood.

The poetry of labor my father taught me in thick timber, axe in hand
splitting firewood, comes to mind in these quiet moments of work.

Emporia

on good days you can smell
the sweet aroma of the Dolly Madison bakery
on bad days you're overwhelmed
by the cruel odor of the meat packing plant

on the worst days they mix together
in a violent concoction of sugar and rot
but luckily the taverns close late and open early
or you wouldn't be able to stand any of it

it's difficult to survive the uncertainty
of long-haul truckers careening past the city at all hours
the screech of the air brakes on their trucks
disturbing the steady hum of highways going other places

all these muddled concerns fade quickly away just outside town
in the rolling blue hills that stretch along a hazy distant horizon

Making Fire

Solid crack of axe striking wood splitting the checks
widen in cold air shatters in echoes off empty trees
bare to the wind and snow sharp on the naked skin
struggle and stack the cordwood balance in the arms.

Hard walk back to warmth and life of the small cabin
dozing in dim early light of thick winter hush and ice
stumble over root and rut, ground crunching underneath,
my jagged breath freezing into thick billowing clouds.

I am quiet at the door so as not to wake you and the child
asleep upstairs, nestled in quilts and still winter morning.
I step into the dim half-light that makes its way inside with me,
also trying to find somewhere warm away from the chill.

In the stove, I rekindle the ends of last night's fire with the new wood;
hot crackle of yellow flame sparks new life the dead of winter.

My Copy of Stafford's Poems

I have dog-eared nearly every yellowed page
of my copy of William Stafford's poetry,
every line of every stanza too important
for me to forget to come back and read again.

Each time my exegesis grows more detailed,
the marginalia beginning to stretch wildly
from one poem to another, the ink
doubling the already sizable weight of the book.

Soon, even the narrow spaces between the lines
will be worked, the deep furrows leaving fertile ground.
My obsessive notation creates a second text,
a palimpsest of my own desperate search for meaning.

Each poem has become a needful request for hesitant reading
and long strolls amid sun-filled air of native trees and tall grasses.

Golem

once the mark of divinity is etched across the forehead
the belly immediately begins filling with dark bile
the liver glows red opening stiff veins with sanguine elasticity
and the chest cavity turns hot in white pulsating flame

the rushing pain of life is marked by an ooze of yellow humors
after an indignant soul, ripped blindly from innocent leisure
is pulled into skin, tight like a beast imprisoned in the joy of meat
the competing interests of transcendence and immanence at play

damp pale eyes lazily slide open searching for cognition
but of course, the mind remains detached
drifting indistinctly over the body in some manner
the philosophers never bothered to define properly

I wonder if this is how we are all thrown into the world surrendering
paradise, a disastrous nativity out of the clay and mud.

Spring in Poland

Spring enters Poland in loud, sudden eruptions
of white linden blooms and green unfolding vines.
The sun, so long a stranger, now hangs around
far past its welcome, after arriving too early.

Rough sand they had used to coat thin snowfalls
now collects into deep drifts along the walkways
and in the corners of every gray building, the wind
takes it up easily into short dust-devils in bare parks.

The cheap tarmac sidewalks start having some bounce
as these warmer days melt them slightly.
By summer, even the soft rubber soles of sneakers
will sink a bit, leaving shallow backwards swooshes behind.

Dawn red blossoms of plum trees break through pavements
shading broken glass and cigarette butts outside the liquor store.

Lament for the Okrąglak

In Poznań there's this building:
a cylindrical, concrete vestige
of communist times, a wonderous
icon of quirky local architecture.

Years ago, strolling through the city,
you could haphazardly wander inside and climb
the double helix of mildly dangerous circular stairs
that wound about, hugging the interior walls.

I remember writing poetry in a drab, makeshift café
at its top, studying the chipped plaster and exposed brick,
lazily looking down over the bare iron rails,
thinking about life and nothing in particular.

Now, for the bottom line, it is become a corporate high-rise devoted
to banks divvying up measly yearly profits and executive benefits.

Gdańsk

you wouldn't think it to look at it
but this city painted in soft pastels
is laden with the weight of history
cursed with the knowledge of the past

even as the crisp salt air of the Baltic
winds its way through tight back alleys
down Long Street past Neptune guarding the Town Hall
to the Golden Gate proclaiming peace and prosperity

the tumult of the last century begs for attention
like the spot that saw the first shots of World War II
or the post office where the SS were fended off
for two weeks by a group of mailmen

it's rather quiet these days now filled with amber-hunting tourists
haggling along the docks, ignoring scars from less certain times

Promised Land, 1975

In the scene—deafening racket of looms
in the background—a vat of chemicals spills,
the barefoot peasant worker covers his nose
but the well-dressed Borowiecki inhales deeply, smiles.

It's a metaphor, you see; the ragged laborer, closer to nature
can't stand the stench of toxic fumes that burn his throat
but the industrialist, a man who has forgotten nature
has become part machine himself, is sustained by poison.

Later his gluttony will seem to get the better of him
audience hoping, believing his greed has brought him to ruin
and they rejoice, until—hard cut—ten years later
we see he's married into the nouveau riche, victorious.

Outside, striking workers are shot; one falls, a red flag in hand
—fade to black—a not so subtle parable, but one worth remembering.

Warsaw

for Jerzy Nasierowski

this city does not lend itself to poetry
in the meat and brick of all its history
Warsaw looms over the Polish sky
defiantly grey and proud

the ghosts of heroes and villains and victims
all tend to forget the deep black lines between them
their palimpsest of blood blending into a thin film
over a thick cement crust that hides very few secrets these days

often I think back to the first time I stumbled
onto Nowy Świat awash in late Spring sunlight
airy chatter of pedestrians echoing off glass shop-fronts
outdoor cafes already full despite the lingering chill

their city has turned into a defiant poem about soot-filled skies
clearing, and blue waters washing away history's muck

All Saints

"He who has never tasted bitterness once,
will never know the sweetness of Heaven."
—Adam Mickiewicz, *Grandfathers' Eve*

Ancestor worship is nothing new;
even long-dead pagans knew enough
to set out feasts for the ghosts of loved ones
at least once a year, toasting to their good health one last time

Some realized there was little difference
between the seen and unseen, that the pellucid line
drifting tentatively between the two worlds
was never enough to stop quick and dead from mingling.

There are others who understood that the deceased turn into gods,
one soul racing to Heaven, the other remaining on Earth
to begin a new life within stone tablets riding atop
the golden shell of a gargantuan tortoise.

Even in this land of stern priests and grandmothers, they've made
a cottage industry of candle wax melted over well-kept tombs.

Oh, Polish Mind, Have You Already Awakened

By Stanisław Wyspiański, April 12, 1905, Kraków
Translated by Jack J. B. Hutchens, Poznań 2021

Oh, Polish mind, have you already awakened?
Weren't you once so fiery and radiant
that from the mere breath of a spirit
you arose like a hundred-armed titan?

Or are you only a longed-for dream, a moment
of comfort over the water of the well, a rare
oasis in uncultured deserts for those camels
that carry your burdens, useful on the journey

only for their strength, but in drought have their insides
opened up so as to drink from their humps as from a spring?
Do your treasures remain undiscovered, or were they simply
destroyed long ago, your pearls picked out through a thick sieve?

Or will we find, in deep waters, a pearl of great wisdom blinding
us with illusions in bright sunlight beneath rivers of filth and grime?

No One Grabs a Button When They see a Chimney Sweep

Ask not the aged; ask the experienced.
     —*Polish proverb*

Are filthy pigeons still the souls of knights forgotten by their king?
Does the future still depend on whether you can stand flat-footed
against a wall that's sinking at a 22-degree angle into the Vistula silt?
Do frogs still pay attention to a fiddlers strumming hypnotic tunes?

No one grabs a button when they see a chimney sweep these days,
even though it was the best advice you could get a hundred years ago.
It's a bad omen when, in a land of myths, old wives' tales
begin losing their power and legends stop being true.

In blue-painted villages, ancient wishing wells are drying up
with desperate longing for randomly tossed copper coins.
The deep granite mountains are empty of sleeping heroes.
The wizard on the moon already sold out for a modern three-
bedroom.

No one bats an eye when storks fly overhead since the mermaid left
town down river, and they forgot to refuel to the fire-breathing dragon.

Lament for Mariupol

It is impossible to get lost in flattened ruins
as grainy char will always point you towards hell,
and tall buildings wavering in the hazy Slavic evening
no longer obstruct violent red horizons.

This long-forgotten place, squeezed between the wide
European plain and the cold deep of the Azov Sea,
is now the stuff of hagiographies recorded on dry
bits of ancient, stained paper falling apart at the seams.

Even the saints regard this jagged martyrdom with awe,
stunned by the brutal pain of concrete brick draping bodies,
their own amateurish suffering a pale analogue soft and dim
against the bright souls of victims shining in afternoon dust.

Rain brings nothing new. Heavy gray drops flood open mouths.
Ash and bone drain into the sea along with the dreams of the dead.

Jack J. B. Hutchens was born and raised in the Flint Hills of Kansas. He attended Emporia State University where he studied poetry under Phil Heldrich and Christopher Howell. After graduation, he lived in Poland for several years, finding a new home there. When he returned, he completed his PhD in Slavic Literatures at the University of Illinois Urbana-Champaign. After teaching Polish literature for several years, he is now a high school teacher of English at Plainfield East High School in Illinois where he lives with his wife Amanda and their daughter Harriet. He is the author of a book of poetry, *There/Here: Poems of Journey and Home*, and a monograph *Queer Transgressions in Twentieth-Century Polish Fiction*.